LZRD

Poems from the Lizard Peninsula

Alyson Hallett
&
Penelope Shuttle

Indigo Dreams Publishing

First Edition: LZRD Poems from the Lizard Peninsula
First published in Great Britain in 2018 by:
Indigo Dreams Publishing Ltd
24 Forest Houses
Halwill
Beaworthy
EX21 5UU
www.indigodreams.co.uk

Alyson Hallett & Penelope Shuttle have asserted their right under the Copyright, Designs and Patents Act 1988 to be identified as the authors of this work.
© 2018 Alyson Hallett & Penelope Shuttle

ISBN 978-1-910834-76-3

British Library Cataloguing in Publication Data. A CIP record for this book can be obtained from the British Library.

This book is sold subject to the condition that it shall not, by way of trade or otherwise, be lent, re-sold, hired out, or otherwise circulated without the authors' and publisher's prior consent in any form of binding or cover other than that in which it is published and without a similar condition including this condition being imposed on the subsequent purchaser.

Designed and typeset in Palatino Linotype by Indigo Dreams.
Author photo of Alyson Hallett by Sean Malyon. Author photo of Penelope Shuttle by Jemimah Kuhfeld.

Cover design by Ronnie Goodyer at Indigo Dreams. Cover image 'Vision in Time III' by Wilhelmina Barns-Graham. Reproduced with kind permission of Wilhelmina Barns-Graham Trust.

Printed and bound in Great Britain by 4edge Ltd.

Papers used by Indigo Dreams are recyclable products made from wood grown in sustainable forests following the guidance of the Forest Stewardship Council.

This book is dedicated to the memory of Peter Redgrove

Of light and stone at the Lizard
　　　the inlife of a community of spirits
　　　　　world interpreted by the dream

from 'Prologue' by Peter Redgrove
(*Visits to the Lizard*, Palores Publications, 2002)

Acknowledgements

Some poems, or versions of them, have already appeared in the following publications: *Raceme; Reliquae; The Honest Ulsterman; Acumen.*

Penny and Alyson would like to thank the days that opened out into great adventures. The Falmouth Hotel for their patience and generosity. The little gold VW car that was gifted to Alyson by Fiona Hamilton – and all the memories of Fiona's mum who travelled in the car with us. The generous ghost of Peter Redgrove. To Robbie Burton for technical support. To Sylvia Miles for additional proof-reading. The strange outcrop of land that is the Lizard for being what it is.

CONTENTS

Lovely Lizard 9
Godspeed 10
Thirteen Practical Reasons for Visiting The Lizard 11
Storm Imogen – 1 12
Storm Imogen – 2 13
Swallows 14
Saint Corantyn 15
The Hospitaller 17
Fish 18
Wallow in silence 19
A Brief Account of Some Parishes on The Lizard 20
Church of the Storms, Gunwalloe 22
Lost 23
24 Sentences for Travellers 24
Dear Serpentine 25
Serpentine Elephant 26
Spring Equinox 2016 27
Rainbow – 1 29
The Weak Road 30
Fig tree, Manaccan Church 31
At Manaccan Church 32
Black 33
Saint Serpentine 34
Lizard Rag 35
At Grade 36
Why Here Why Not 37
Named Storm 38
Grade Church 40
Hum 41
Tusk 42
What Do Waves Do All Day? 43
Lzrd 44
Candles for the Well 45
what is this strange flower 46
Lizard Bible 47

A Piece of Serpentine 48
St Keverne 49
Cury: Tuesday Afternoon Prayers 50
Village Church 51
If there were fifty or more words for sea 52
Bells of St Cury 53
The Lizard is better than a horn spoon that will hold forty peas 54
Cleaning the Well 55
Terra Arida 56
St Ruan Minor 57
The Boys 58
Kynance Cove 59
Dolphin Ditty 60
Surprise!!! 61
Rough Angels 62
Landewednack 63
rainbow – 2 65
sapphires in a monarch's crown 66
Sunday Lizard 67
Lizard's Perfect Pitch 68
Lizard 69

NOTES 71
Postscript 1 72
Postscript 2 74
The Lizard: A Geographer's View 77

LZRD

Poems from the Lizard Peninsula

Lovely Lizard

how can I be satisfied
with a serpentine pebble
on a table on a balcony in Somerset
when Kynance Grade Manaccan
rival every other place light plops down on?

Godspeed

God's in these wheels and she's turning so fast
she's a dervish in black spinning us into the ecstasy
of travel, this way we have of zooming from a to b
thinking we're just driving when all the while she's
there beneath us like good soil beneath a plant,
hidden in the Goodyear tyre or the cheapest available
that I bought last time I had a puncture. Who'd have
thought she'd make her church in a place like this? Who'd
have thought these drives are holy acts, that each inch
of the journey is sacred? Through the windscreen we spy
a spit of land leaning into the Atlantic while the swan
of all journeys stretches her wings beneath us.

Thirteen Practical Reasons for Visiting The Lizard

To check-out every mischief-saint of the peninsula
To dowse your doubt
To raise your spirits   one by one
To discourse with the summer Hassidim
To hoot the owl   to comprehend the pilchard
To hear laughter from the well-house
To pause on the road, listening for it again
To clean-slate your life
To call the life-boat your friend
To trust the wheat field to take you in the right direction
To remember your dead
To hold court with the living

Storm Imogen – 1

not the wind-crazed stagger across
Church Cove
or bombs of water
that explode on the beach

not the spectacular sandpiper
piping the edge of a boiling sea
or post-smash spray
devilling cliffs and caves

not the way we double over
and break into the gale like thieves
or the punch punch punch
of sea on sand

but a cafe in Porthleven
where a frenzy of harbour-
bound waves pixelates
the swirling town

and makes me sea-sick
even though I'm warm indoors
and sitting firmly
down

Storm Imogen – 2

The storm comes to wake us.
Shake us. Berate us.

Ho-Hoa, it says. Jibberdy-doo, it says. Ho-Hoa.

A cliff loses its legs.
Stones fly, tiles fly, birds smash into walls.

Ho-Hoa, it says, Jibberdy-doo.

Storm Imogen presses its face to my face.
Stares in. Invades.

Ho-Hoa, it says. Jibberdy-doo.

A wave snaps a boat,
likes the sound, snaps thirty more.

Ho-Hoa, it says. Jibberdy-doo.

The storm comes to wake us.
Shake us. Berate us.

Ho-hoa, it says. Jibberdy-doo, it says. Ho-Hoa.

Swallows

The sea has everything and nothing on its blue mind
as it strokes The Lizard's tail. The sea has a hill full of lighthouses,
a lifeboat sleeved in every cove. The sea never tries to be different,
turns its tides one by one, blue and green, green and blue.
Swallows teem above the cliff, squeaking, cheeping, flitting.
They dip down to the salt as if to cormorant-dive,
then scoot right up into high blue.
But the sea goes along in its furrows, content with the magic of water,
while the birds keep all the magic of air.

Faster than sight or sorrow, the swallows clip the sky,
remembering Saint Wynwallow when she was garmented in feathers and air.

Saint Corantyn

gives me a snowdrop posy
a chunk of storm
a church built on sand

gives me the past
in the shape
of a village with five names

On Shrove Tuesday
he leaves me
(to my own surprise) well-shriven

Corantyn
hands me a prayer book
its pages in deliberate wrong order

offers me hail
a gargoyle's grin
and a nudge in the ribs

Saint Corantyn gives me Antioch
all of the kit
and most of the caboodle

my ship coming in
my gold turned back to straws
blowing along the poverty road

He gives me white-hot truth
hidden in a stone-cold lie
Quimper Cathedral on the palm of his hand

He bails out my grave
He guides me
through the stone doorway

with its chevron
and pellet enrichments
to the nook shafts and the jambs

He writes me into his journal of dowsing
takes me fathoms deep
to old forests of oak, willow and hazel

gives me his freshwater blessing
sends me on my way
riddling

The Hospitaller
    St Corantyn's Church, Cury

Welcome, the hospitaller says,
    offering tea and Breakaway biscuits.

She lights a candle in a scallop shell,
    unspools the thread of old Celtic

prayers – how we'll chat then stand, hand
    in hand and turn in circles –

she listens in a way that lets us
    spare no detail – gammy knee,

dad who died six months ago,
    last night's wild sheet-lightning storm

then fifteen hours without power
    and all the meat

in the freezer gone rotten –
    round and round we go

the hospitaller guiding us
    through our harmless repetitions

as we turn hand in hand
    to keep the Celtic flame alive

to keep it pumping through
    stones and blood and sky-

Fish

I am the fish
I am miraculous,

the saint's daily snack,
sustenance of a holy man

He gnaws my flesh to sushi
but I live

What he consumes of me
renews at once,

my scales glittering whole
Brother Saint, feed on me, I'm your daily fish

No swan of freshwater or salt
offers you wing or breast to devour

No ripe figs fall into your mouth
It is I, Fish, on whom you feast,

your soul's delicious consort

Wallow in silence
   at Gunwalloe

A Brief Account of Some Parishes on The Lizard

If the parish of Grade has griffons
let them be rampant
let there be three of them at that grim spot

If the parish of Ruan Major has vestments
let them be made of tawny silk from Venice,
sheer as a Red Lion's eyelash

If the parish of Ruan Minor alias St Rumon in Morrep
has marriages
let that parish also have its deaths by standing stone
and its births in the midnight

If a parish has the right
to graze one horse on a certain field in a neighbouring parish
let no other parish dispute it

If in our parishes we bear names
let them be old names with no Saxon blood,
Jacka, Bray, Hocken, Roskilly,
earth names of The Lizard

If we have churches, and who can dispute the fact,
let them stand their granite and serpentine
both high and low
on The Lizard

And that horse we mentioned before?
Let it carry a bonus of sheaves on its back,
as many as it can carry in a day from that field

If our parishes have bell-chambers
let them be hung with sweet ringers, tenor-voiced
across The Lizard

If in the parish of Grade we have a relic of The Holy Cross
let that splinter be brought home
from The Holy Land by the pilgrim Sir Roger Whalesborough
hidden miraculously in his thigh

And if in any parish here in Terra Arida
we find doors for The Devil
let them be so small only a young griffon
or trainee demon may slip their mischief through

Church of the Storms, Gunwalloe

I brought the stump of a candle
to the Church of the Storms and lit it.
Its light flared for as long as there
was wax to eat, wick to burn.

I listened to the last light as it bugled
its flame over granite, as it tucked
itself into vestigial pockets of air.
When it was gone it was still there –

in vestigial pockets of air, in quartz-
pocked stone. I brought the stump
of a candle to the Church of the Storms
and sent my father into the waves

from which he'd come. Who knows
what this means – I'm a particle
of pure incomprehension.
The Church of the Storms doesn't care.

It takes the stump of a candle
lets it have its final exuberant flare.

Lost

The first time the Lizard
gives us its lostness
each road circles back on itself,
each sign signals
somewhere we want to go
but can never reach.

The second time
the roads begin to feel like sugar
folded into whisked
egg whites, the way they blend
into each other until there's no
distinguishing.

The third time we look
forward to being lost,
abandon maps and meet
everything as if it's meant
to be this way and no other –

gulls, pinking thrift,
Orthodox Jews on holiday,
pasties, hedgerows, grumpy
waitress, chips, sea –
all fluted with light and tucked
under the Lizard's lovely wing.

24 Sentences for Travellers

When you meet a swan offer the creature all your worldly goods.
Your body is your boat: attend to it and hope for wind in your sails.
As you travel, listen for the echo's next-of-kin.
Friends can take many shapes – human, animal, plant, insect.
Never underestimate the power of a saint to call god no more than
                                                    'a flash in the pan'.
Enlist the help of ghosts.
Marry a Lizard girl and you marry the entire peninsula.
When it rains porridge, the poor traveller has no spoon.
When the blind man leads the way across The Lizard, woe to those who follow.
When all your food's gone, eat the bark of the white pine – it's high in vitamin C.
The world rests on the tip of the tongue, even on The Lizard.
Take a pebble from the weak road, a stone from the strong path, place one in
                                          your left shoe, the other in your right.
Learn to accept gifts you didn't expect to be given.
Sometimes getting lost is the only way.
The barefoot path is the path to trust but when shadow is crowned
                                        King of The Lizard, stand still, bow down.
Your body is a tuning fork – listen to its sounds.
On The Lizard, we get nowhere fast, like lab kangaroos on a treadmill.
Everything we forget, The Lizard remembers.
When you have no words, let your hands do the talking.
Enemies can take many shapes – human, animal, plant, insect.
When The Lizard turns dark and harsh, like all its shipwrecks
        or the day's rolling newscast, pray for the intercession of Saint Corantyn.
A white gull's feather resting on the scales of the wind is a good omen,
                                                    so they say in Gunwalloe.
When a woman in a bakery in Tirana touches her hand to her heart
                                        it changes the shape of everything to come.
When thunder gathers in folds of light, do not pick a quarrel with anyone.

Dear Serpentine

what made you come to the Lizard,
you who are unlike all others in Cornwall,

no kith or kin in Britain? What made you
leave brothers in the Antigorio Valley,

sisters on Mount Olympus, countless aunts
and uncles in Quebec? Dearest,

was your course determined by earthquakes
or the most common thirst of all,

the need to move? Adored by Aztecs, named
for your likeness to snake's skin, some say

you blaze through the spine like fire.
Dear Serpentine, you set off with no boots,

no boat, no friends – and here we are
sunning and swimming on your migrant shores.

Serpentine Elephant

His trunk is a kindly serpent,
he shrugs it over his shoulder
chic and casual as you like,
as befits a keystone species.

He's the red of rampage,
polished till he's fit for a queen.

1846: The Lizard:
Victoria steps from her royal yacht
(The Victoria and Albert paddle steamer)
to be enchanted by serpentine in all its facets.

From then on (they say) the royal Kundalini never slept.

In her wake
serpentine factories sprang up,
making obelisks, dogs, and other trinkets.
But best of all are you,

elephant igneous and metamorphic,
neither gabbro nor basalt,
superior of course to volcanic ash,
royally-rich in memory

of the Variscan orogeny,
not bush or forest elephant,
but Lizard elephant.

Spring Equinox 2016

Every wind in the compass absent without leave,
returning light the quietest grey possible
on a day when The Meneage holds its breath,
a day of three flowerless churches…

Prosperous St Keverne with graves for the drowned,
aisle pillars set on gnarly bedrock of serpentine and granite
as if the church had burst up
from underground, complete with ghost wall-paintings
of one-eyed St Christopher and red and gold glass St Cecilia

A weak road along Gillan Creek leads us to St Anthony,
his smaller plainer church,
attendant swans sipping nearby from the freshwater stream on the beach
Inside (count them!) two Last Suppers,
the first carved in black bog oak,
medieval figures vehement and heart-sore,
the second a 3D Victorian representation dull as ditchwater,
but in both pieces Judas sneers in the background,
knife concealed in his hand…
Nearby, a candle-lit list of the Vicars of this Cure unfolds
its beautiful calligraphy until the present day

On the hilly graveyard, silver christmas baubles
still decorate
an evergreen tomb tree,
looking back at the tower you'll see a busy boatyard
rubbing shoulders with the church,
the holy well hugged by bushes, stone lintel just visible,
and a glimpse of water flowing down to a swan-liked stream

Along the creek path, a faint green-mist of budding branches lines the banks…

The rising tide turns us back and on to Manaccan,
dedicated to an unknown saint, where
after two hundred and fifty years
the old fig-tree still spurts with miraculous force
from the stone flank of the church

We count its first few unfurling green leaves
as the older yews look on
knowing that bad luck comes to all who pick and eat the fruit

It was here, of course, during the Napoleonic wars,
that the famous Captain Bligh was arrested
while carrying out research
for the Admiralty in the Helford River
and locked in a coal cellar for a spy –
eventually he proved his identity,
became good friends with his captor Rev'd Polwhele

Today inside Manakneu Church
(where a long-past vicar discovered titanium)
the Lord's Prayer murmurs in Cornish all day long
– *Agan Tas ni, usi y'n nev*

Rainbow – 1

After tea in the Black Swan
we drive up Gweek's steep hill
and look right to see the dirt catch

fire in a field filled with
shorn stems of wheat
the sun furious as it shimmies down

the trunks of trees
to seize each drop of rain and bend it
bow it round the nape of Cornwall's neck.

Never before has such a rainbow
been seen – each colour so violently bright
it trembles and shakes –

we lean forward and watch it
blaze and blaze
for nine whole miles without a break.

The Weak Road

Swerve right to St Anthony's Bay.
Take the weak road
and hug the inlet's edge
as trees swoop on the left
and on the right fall away.
The weak road's a thin road,
it needs vigilance, diligence,
vehicles that are light.
Peaky waves
play on the creek's blue back,
two swans paddle
faster than we can drive.
On and on, all of us
as weak and strong as we
can be. The swans
arrive first, smug
and swanly as they preen
on see-through
water. We slink into St Anthony's
church, increasingly aware
of our church addiction.
What weaklings we are!
A strip of bog oak seizes us,
roots us in the throttle of its gaze –
whoever carved this last supper
made each person so real,
so achingly detailed
neither of us would be surprised
if Christ upped-sticks and walked away.

Fig tree, Manaccan Church

sweet fig
        how do you suck sap from stone
        and make mid-air your home

sweet fig
        you defy every known law
        and appear to grow straight out of a wall

sweet fig
        is that a saint I see shouldering your weight
        or does this Lizard air make us dream awake

At Manaccan Church

Famous old figtree
        rooted and flourishing
on the tower wall –
        green badge on grey sleeve
Inside you see the roots
        congregating
and how the angel-chaperoned Christ
        in the east,
severe, bearded à la Russe,
        watches the stone aisles
approach, recede
        Saint Manacca
in bright glass
        holds her church
on the palm of her hand
        Over there
a memorial tablet – *died in Cannes*
        Lamb of worn stone
above the south door's zigzag
        and near the porch
the blood-red crane's bill
        spilling
her sanguinary summer
        at the foot
of the ecclesiastical fig
        even unto the hyssop
that springeth out of the wall

Black

There have been blacks before.
Jet. Obsidian. Granite. Coal black,
peat black, brownish-brackish
blackbird's wing black. Pupil black
(which isn't really black but a hole
to darken a hidden red retina).
Malcolm X black, black-slippered
newts, black patent shoes. Rat black,
black belt, black dog of depression.
None like this though: all blacks,
including the All Blacks, are unlike
serpentine black shot through with red.

Saint Serpentine

Saint Serpentine speaks his word   in red iron
and green sea-water   Bless us Saint Serpentine
with your cold fingers   and fiery heart
Your saint's mantle of rock-slide and mudstone
is polished to a shine by your saint thoughts and deeds
Bless us Saint Serpentine   Preach us the good news
of tectonic activity and debris fall   Bring us word of the Pleistocene
and of The Tertiary   Promise us native gold   Pray for us the crowbar prayer
Baptize us with quartz-rich dust   Bless us Saint Serpentine
We'll lay salad burnet   dwarf rush   five-winged orchids on your portable altar
Let us not complain you never fought with a dragon
were never invited to Canterbury   Bless us Saint Serpentine
We do not ask your hands be Anglo-Saxon hands   dear hands of our saint
washed down to us by ancient rivers and the land's love   Bless us

Lizard Rag
> *For P*

forgotten days of our Lizard
where the moon's a country madcap

where our time-ball of mistakes
glitters in safe-hiding forever

where our love life replays
in the swoon and swoop of Lizard clouds

even in double-winter years
and springs ruled by the Greek church

Lizard – where our constant servant
is an endless red sunset on a rainy summer evening

Who's Who of The Lizard remembers you

At Grade

The long green path comes to Grade
where the mist turns round

where the field falls away
where the altar offers dust and dry leaves

where the lectern shines its serpentine –
berry-red, blood-red –

where the seamark tower's leaf-ridden and frail

Wet salt air has nibbled away its soul
and its cement – its bells untongued

The long green path walks away from Grade
mists drift ahead…between…beyond

Why Here Why Not

They say it's better to be buried
on the other side of the church.
There's a faster path to heaven,
more angels to winch you up.

Dead is dead I say and who needs
to fat a church already brimmed
with gold, windows winnowed
to transparency or painted

with the rich lord's name, Vyvyan?
Ground is down and so is gravity.
I'll take my last chance where
most are too frightened to come:

the dark side of the church, seaward,
on Grade's prehistoric mound. If anyone
asks of my stone why here, I'll carve
both question and answer clear.

Named Storm

1

When you go
to The Church of the Storms
best go on a day
when a storm called Imogen
is rough-riding the bucking tide
of Dollar Cove

Go to the church lying-low
in the flank of the sand-hills
on a day of ice rain
and gull flurry

White waves rear up
teem down in a rush
towering walls of a salt city
built of storm's shove and shudder

    great white spume-shoulders
    set to the wheel of the storm

Go there on a day
when you can't hear yourself speak
and only the tiny shorebirds
can dodge the pounding fists of the wave
(even a gull gets sucked-up into the storm's maw)

Go there when horizontal rain
bullets your face with its fusillade
    when the sea's
      in a towering rage
and with a friend who loves storms,
the sea biffing and bashing the cliffs,
not even the royal ravens
can stop it

2

Then turn your back
on the boom and boil and bubble of it
The gale will scud you up the beach
in a minute
hurtle you
over the salt-bitten bridge
and along the muddy track
to the church behind its tamarisk hedge

Bell tower standing all on its ownsome

The storm can't set foot in the Church of Storms
at Gunwalloe near and far
Its stone walls silence Imogen
Wooden rafters and granite pillars
hold up more than the roof

Three pilgrim bibles
open on the side altar speak
three silences,
English, French, Spanish

When you're closed-in there
slip yourself down
into Gunwalloe's silence
one of those wells of silence
the world keeps safe
off its beaten tracks

*

ps
Make sure you go there when
they've got
the fire roaring
at The Halzephron Inn

Grade Church

Unloved church
hard-to-love church
frowning Lord on your mound
above the treeless tableland

    What's easier to love
    is the path arrow-straighting
    through yellow wheat
    a bevy of day-moths and dragonflies
    biffing along the hedge of unripe blackberries
    a stranger with her dog

But Grade
austere old stone flagon
you're hard to love
though god knows we try

Hum

Returning through the wheat,
I catch a humming in my ear,
touch the telegraph pole planted in the field,
shocked by the power coursing through the wood,
electricity rip-roaring to itself,
Prometheus Bound,
rippling sinews of it under my hand,
like my lover.

Tusk

A track clean trod towards a church is clean trod away from it too.
A path goes two ways always. Slap bang in the middle of this one
there's a splintering pole, a tusk of wood soaring up.

Away from the church at Grade the path takes a downhill tilt
which makes our treading feet go faster. Down the trodden row we go,
the two-ways path our mentor. Penny stops

while I go on, the rush of air behind suddenly emptier without her.
Turn then turn again – is that really her, stock still, two hands pressed
to the pole?

There you are I say as I trot back along the two-way path shrinking the hollow
between us. What are you doing I want to ask but you can tell
when asking's not a good idea and so I stand stock still too.

Taking note of the smile on her face I bend my knees a bit and relax,
stare out to sea, suddenly aware of a breeze hula-hulaing through the field.

Truth to tell, she says later, when we've finished the trot along the tilting
two-way path to the stile at the end and climbed over it, truth to tell
I was plugged into a fizz, a buzz of pure electric.

What Do Waves Do All Day?

climb so high
they coat the stars with salt

tickle the feet
of small brown birds
as they tinker around in spume

squeeze through gaps in mortar
to dampen bibles
on the Church of the Storms' altar

execute wave origami
on adverts pinned to a porch
each corner curling inwards

sneak into arthritic bones
to make them ache and moan
like glockenspiels of pain

stand on each other's backs
then topple down
inside their broken spumy crowns

Lzrd

you interloper

you wastrel
you coil around my heart

Lzrd

you squeezer of vowels from words

you limpet
you crazy misfit Cornish wonder

Lzrd

you wizard you witch

wildflower magnet
we can't resist

Candles for the Well

We found candles in a plastic box left there by The Well Master.
The igniter was empty, we couldn't light our two candles,
didn't want to go back to the village Spar for matches,
reluctant to break our link with the old well in its bare stone shed.

Down the serpentine hedge-steps came a couple and their dog.
The man was a smoker, he loaned us his lighter.
Our candle flames held steady at the well side.
There we stood, four strangers drawn to the ancient spring.

I felt dreamy, noticing nothing but the flames and the water.
Alyson tells me later how the woman suddenly murmured a name,
blew a kiss into the air. The man did the same.
The woman said to him, it's made me cry again.

Off they went across the cloudy field.

what is this strange flower
        pawing at my feet
                this weed this serpentine creeper?

Lizard Bible

> *we must ask for what we want*
> *so the world can take pleasure*
> *in giving it to us*

so says the bible of the Lizard
where one hazy day leans
into the next –

at St Grade's Well
three serpentine steps
take us from road
to field
where candles without matches
sit tight in a plastic box
by the water's side –

I ask a passing stranger
for a light
and he fetches a flame
from his pocket –

the bible of the Lizard
writes in a language
so cool and clear
Penny's moved to quote Auden –

thousands have lived without love,
not one without water…

**A Piece of Serpentine
Washed-up on Maenporth Beach**

handed to me by a friend in a Falmouth back street
she reached in her bag   gave me the red stone
found on her morning run
the stone brims cool in my hand   very holdable
its broad weighty splendour   the darkest red can be
before   it must be called black

Matrix of serpentine   shadings of blue-grey in the red
green mottles   flecks and inclusions
a hair-thin vein of white quartz at the mid-point
half-circling the stone
sitting on my hand   in stony seizin

I hold it at arm's length
now the white quartz is a waterfall seen from miles away
the red shine dulls away
then quickens in midsummer light
serpentine visitor   found so unexpectedly
at Maenporth   where the cliffs are made of golden galena

Smooth and pitted   mountain's cousin
one thousand times removed
rolled and scoured
along the coast by wave after wave
castaway pounded by salt-water fists
all the way from The Lizard   to Maenporth's holiday-home sands

St Keverne

After porridge get in your car
and drive to St Keverne.
Park in the church-shadowed square,
walk down past sun-spattered
fields to a stream.

See how light stretches
its thin blue tongue
over stones and water.
How trees
stride into the sky
and soil sinks around
the tunnels of worms.

Who knows what happens
to you when you walk
here – you return home
changed and unchanged,
something soft, like the cough
of an angel, lodged
between your ribs.

Cury: Tuesday Afternoon Prayers

In the February dark
In the February freeze
Six women in a circle
Six women drinking tea

St. Corantyn below
St. Corantyn above
St. Corantyn beside us
St Corantyn our love

Six women in a circle
Six women holding hands
Six women turning clockwise
Six women of the land

St. Corantyn below
St. Corantyn above
St. Corantyn beside us
St Corantyn our love

Six women turning clockwise
Six women making prayers
A church of celtic stones
A church of celtic air

St. Corantyn below
St. Corantyn above
St. Corantyn beside us
St Corantyn our love

Village Church

In the Lady Chapel
the women pray
in a strange chatty way
hard to tell chat from prayer
not a seamless but an interrupted praying
sharing burdens
the aunt/neighbour with her infected leg
six months wait for her hospital appointment
the child taken to Manchester for a brain scan
St George leaning down from the window
with his clear blue gaze
his blue-green tunic
his beautifully worked sword
and subdued red dragon
The praying stops and starts
wanders along chattily
the stubby candle-flames wriggling
then steadying as if in league
with the women's voices
praying or gossiping every
Tuesday afternoon
for the grief of the village
and the world

If there were fifty or more words for sea
I'd use the one that means Screaming Sea as a title

force your way to the beach
through a juggernaut wind
sinksink sand
and there she is enraged
in foam-rimmed grey

all the steel in the world
couldn't stop her
no stone or saint
strong enough
to resist her stallion kick

she swallows a gull
    it's not a party trick
guns her spray
vomits her tarantella
into the vortices of day

she doesn't care
she's eaten ships
cliffs trees
her appetite's endless
and that's just her way

Bells of St Cury

When the Priest Husband
of the future Mother Charlotte
stepped out of history
to stroke my hair
my aura shone from here to Carnmenellis
and the world zinged sideways
in the vortex of my adoration

but none of this
is mentioned in the Inquisition of 1294
nor is there any record
of that spring morning
in any year you like to name
when St Corantyn
peered down from heaven

at the six named bells of his church,
Praise, Thanksgiving,
Prayer, Faith,
Hope and Charity,
(loved also by Arthur Conan Doyle),
and noted,
out of the corner of his saint eye,

not the Heart Moth nor the Scarce Vapourer
but the Black Mullein, *verbascum nigrum*,
fluttery lover of churchyards and tomb-grass.

The Lizard is better than a horn spoon that will hold forty peas

Beneath The Lizard　　　　　　is a crystalline basement
It was made by ocean closures　　　　and the mischiefs of shelf seas
　　　o shallow-water marine sands and silts
　　　　o simplified geological map of The Lizard Complex
Noah thought about building the Ark for five hundred years
he took six hundred to build it　　　　The Lizard scorns such haste
　　　o time's hand of blood and bone
　　　o mineralization　　　o fragment of ocean lithosphere
I will not come theirin to daye　　cried Noah's wife, spurning the Ark
Come in, wife, in twentye devilles ways!　　　begged Noah
holding the dove by a string over the edge of the Ark for three hundred years
　　　　The Lizard yawns at such brevity　　　O Ghosts of Avalonia

Cleaning the Well

A screw of silver paper
a drowned snail
a bunch of plastic anemones
Alyson leans in to scoop them out
of the field corner shrine
tucked-in square of cold dark sweet water
housed in serpentine vestments
rough blocks with one edge rubbed
to a reddish shine by the pilgrim hand
No padlocked gate bars the well
(as shown in the 1922 photo guidebook)
so we can kneel on the serpentine kerb
of the water-chantry
wondering at water's long incumbency
A Virgin/Naiad statuette
presides in the shadow-niche
alongside some shade-loving long-leaved greenery
water parsnip? water hemlock?
sprouting from the far corner
of this green retreat
welcoming everyone who wishes to be welcomed

Terra Arida

Words spoken here
are made from Mondays, Wednesdays and Saturdays of the sea
and the wheeling manors of the winds

Here your half-brother is the life of St Rumon,
your under-sister the keeper of the school-pence

Springs and wells of this land are revered,
they are also our old friends
The civil parishes dance by moonlight across the glebe lands
in defiance of *the iniquity of our late disturbed times*

Terra Arida is neither Magna or Parva,
it lives on square-mile wheat and barley,
bells stung into tolling
by daylight brighter than coffins of red porphyry

St Ruan Minor

In a tiny village
sits a tiny church,
its tiny tower covered
in reddening ivy.
A tiny lichen city sprawls
along the branches
of a tree, crab apples
shiny as newly-lit
street lamps. Tiny steps
take us almost
nowhere as we stop
to listen to the slow
hush hush of a broom
brushing a brick-stoned
yard. The sound shakes us
down, readies us for
the church of St Ruan:
porch so low we touch
its roof with our tiny
hands before stepping
into its glove of wood
and stone and kneelers.

The Boys

Light hearts of the sky
wing-whirling the little old church round and round
topsy-turvying altar
tarot-ish stained glass windows
spinning the minikin tower like a top
till the serpentine blocks beg for mercy

At last the church steadies,
stands grounded
as the graveyard's lichened crab-apple
with its windfall train of harsh red fruit
or the two dead boys
who watch from February and December 1917

The tower hides its thought in ivy
A cloud darkens the sky like a little Viking
A saintly eye of air and stone is looking at this moment forever

Who can meet that gaze in quiet St Ruan's land?

Kynance Cove

I'll tell you
nothing
of Kynance
except
that Penny's
National Trust
card saved us
a five pound
parking fee
and that while
she sat
on a bench
with fish carved
into it
overlooking
the sea
I clambered
down
a steep path
and disappeared
into the smoke
and incense
of Serpentine

Dolphin Ditty

Admiral Font sang up his dolphins four
the dolphins dear to his heart

He heaved them up by their wooden tails
o those swimmers he knew so well

Zig me your zags and zag me your zigs
sang Admiral Font to his dolphins

Shiver m'timbers   my holy-water lovelies
belay   belay   belay

Font full of sea   seadog full of brandy
That's what I saw above Kynance

White sail of a sermon   anchor of a prayer
That's what I saw with the jolly old Admiral

Font full of brandy   prayer full of dolphins
That's what I saw above Kynance

Surprise!!!

The big double-decker Redruth-bound bus
is a surprise as we round the corner of tiny Ruan Minor

and so (a few hours later) is the Regent Cafe at Lizard Green
full to the gunwales of fish-and-chippers –

and when I open the door
their forty pairs of cold-fish eyes stare us out that door

Rough Angels
Landewednack Church

Porch-angels hacked from wood,
not carved,
but made by urgent hands, sans skill

Driftwood angels the tide has gifted,
then discarded

Worm-eaten angels
who harbour birds' nests
as roughly made as themselves,
as instinctively made

Landewednack

1

Up from the sea's swell, along
from the picture-perfect house
and the shack where serpentine
was polished and sold, away from
the famous coast path, in from
the steep road, the crow road, the road
that's shy of cars even in August:
Landewednack.

2

Church porch
of a poor woman's
dream – serrated Vs,
spirals, crosses in circles.

No sign of blood
just echoes of sun
and moon and
yew berry.

3

Inside the church a huge bell squats on a wooden plinth
looking as if the surrounding church
has been made for it.

4

Peter said each church
had its own particular silence

as if silences are various,
as if John Cage might always be on tour
with a performance of 4'33"

5

I sit on a hand-sewn
kneeler in a silence
so warm it melts
the walls of the church
and sends my body spinning
over the sea without
uprooting an ounce of me
from the cup of the sawn
and sandpapered pew.

6

Lizard. Britain's most southerly tip –
home to pilchard, chough, shipwreck.

Lizard. The last place –
last as in lasting and last as in final.

Lizard. Still ringing with the last-heard
sermon preached in Cornish in 1670.

7

The past prepares us for
future ghosts, rain, confetti

a lifting of Lyonesse
from the sea's cold jetty.

rainbow – 2

exit the black swan
        and let the gods who hide in cars
                haul you to the top of a hill

where you glance into
        the heart of a stubbled field
                blazing with late light

a sky glistened
        with bolts of shimmering silk
                so bright they're almost blinding

you count every colour
        of the rainbow rising up
                then curving down

then count again the rainbow's
        double, its little back-up pal
                echoing whatever song a rainbow

sings as you drive the b-road
        back to falmouth eyes split
                between sky and ground

sapphires in a monarch's crown
envy Lizard's blue day

Sunday Lizard

slips into the beak
of a small brown bird
as it searches for holes in the wind

>advertises *Grave Concerns*
>a business that cares for graves
>you're too busy to tend

sneaks into the hands
of grass cutters
the stems of daisies

>disguises itself as a stone
>dedicated to Hilda and Hilda

plays with grey granite pillars
as they lean to one side
like old drunks

>shoves us rain-tattered and wind-battered
>into a pub –
>>heaven is the Halzephron Inn

Lizard's Perfect Pitch

The ground puts its ear to the air
        bird echo
        wave smack
        insect patter

The sea puts its ear to the sky
        cloud mumble
        heartbeat horizon
        vapour trail's thunder

The year puts its ear to the day
        thistle rustle
        wheat-speech
        teazel and barley and heather songs
        the great white bride-struck lilies along the path to Church Cove, sighing

The old bee of summer puts an ear to sun
        hears his own hummmmmmmmmmmmmmmmmmmmm

Lizard

we will ride your back again
great lizard beast

we will climb into my golden VW
and pootle from Falmouth

to St Keverne,
Manaccan, Kynance,

we'll burrow
beneath your scales

gobble ripe figs,
guzzle your salt-scratched air

Lizard we'll ride you
as Kaleesi rides her dragons

seasoned hearts and seasoned eyes
beneath your spindled-lizard skies

NOTES

Saint Corantyn:
Patron saint of St Cury Church. Originally a hermit, he lived upon a miraculously-renewing fish. He later became Bishop of Truro, then Bishop of Quimper in Brittany.

24 Sentences for Travellers:
This poem was inspired by the following from A Handbook of the Cornish Language: 'The Cornish conversations in Andrew Borde's Booke of the Introduction of Knowledge, [was] printed in 1542. These consist of the numerals and twenty-four sentences useful to travellers.' Jenner, Henry (Printed by Amazon) p.19.
Some of Penelope's sentences are adapted from traditional proverbs.

Bells of St Cury:
The tombs of Revd William Broadley (vicar 1843-1855) and his wife (Mother Maria Charlotte) can be found not at Cury Church but at Carnmenellis Church. The Rev. Broadley (The Priest Husband) had previously been Vicar of St Cury. Maria Charlotte Broadley (Mother Charlotte) wished to provide a church for the outlying hamlet of Four Lanes but her husband died and she moved elsewhere. She became Mother Superior of the Sisterhood of St Peter's, Vauxhall, London, and is commemorated by a plaque in Pencoys church placed there in 1977 as part of the celebrations of the centenary of the Diocese of Truro. St Cury Churchyard is a conservation haven for the Black Mullein moth. The bells of St Cury are named as given in the above poem.

The Lizard is better than a horn spoon that will hold forty peas:
Italicized phrases in this poem are quotations from *Noah (Chester Miracle Plays)*.

Terra Arida:
The villages of Ruan Minor and Grade are in an isolated corner of The Lizard. As early as 1470 they were described as 'Terra Arida' or 'The Barren Lands'.

Dolphin Ditty:
The lid of the font at Landewednack Church is decorated with four carved dolphins.

Postscript 1

One morning, standing in Penny's kitchen, we heard warnings about Storm Imogen on the radio. The weather forecaster advised everyone to stay indoors and not make any journeys unless absolutely necessary. Penny and I looked at each other. There was a glint in her eye. We fetched waterproof coats and laced up our walking shoes. Without a word, we both knew we wanted to head off to the Lizard to see the power and the fury, to immerse ourselves in sea spray and winds so strong we might not be able to stand up.

A couple of months after that first exhilarating trip to the Lizard, we went again. Something drew us there, an invisible thread pulling us towards Helston and then indicating left, past Goonhilly and on to the peninsula of land whose foundation stone of serpentine is not to be found anywhere else in the UK.

After the first journey, Penny said she had written some poems. I hadn't written anything – but after the third visit a few poems came pushing through. Maybe we could write a pamphlet together Penny suggested. I thought this was a great idea – but then the poems kept coming and within months we had a book-sized manuscript between us.

The first co-edit of work took place in the Falmouth Hotel. We settled onto a sofa in the morning and stayed until evening. We had morning coffee, lunch, afternoon tea. People came and went. A wedding happened next door. The sky lightened and darkened and the sea tried on different shades of grey and blue. We were a fixed point in a swirling pool, piles of paper on the carpet at our feet, the staff sashaying along every now and then to clear empty cups and glasses and plates.

Editing together was different to editing poems for a sole-authored book. We were plumbing the strata of our friendship and our work as if they were inseparable – which in many ways they are. It's a rare and delicious thing to be able to edit together so honestly and consistently, although I know this is something that Penny often shared with her late husband, Peter Redgrove.

We thought of him often as we travelled and worked. He was a guardian angel, a presiding presence. In many ways he was a third collaborator in all our journeys and subsequent scribblings.

There's only one co-written poem, '24 Sentences for Travellers'. The rest are written by one or the other of us, but who can say what difference travelling together made to what we then wrote? Any experiment is influenced by the ingredients that go into making it. The ground of this experiment was informed by the warmth of friendship, sharing of stories, an awareness that's fostered by two pairs of eyes and ears being tuned to the world outside, inside and in between.

LZRD acknowledges the deep generosity that exists between fellow writers – those who are dead as well as alive. For all of this, and the support of the strong community of writers in Falmouth, I am deeply thankful.

A.H.

Postscript 2

Going Behind the Appearance of Things

The breakers pumping fine spray
    into the cliff air like spinnerets
        creating cinemas of mist.
Gates, trees and a long wall.
    Not milking
        but silking the spider
Called the Silver Weaver.
    A Lizard spider on a warm rock:
        seven different silks
From seven different glands,
    bullet-proof spider silk.
        Moments of silk.
The Lizard,
    all restored and in place there,
        a silver tree that led us
To a stone well; a whitebeam
    turning silver in the breeze
        as though it were filling with water;
Rolled into silver as though
    the contents of the well
        were a tree spinning silk.
Two gulls,
    flying across the cliff-face,
        shifted its immense gaze.

In his poem *Spiderous Lizard*, quoted above, Peter Redgrove, my late husband, captures the way that part of Cornwall 'restored' us on every visit. I well remember the shivering tree silver with light, the power and significance The Lizard had for us in our life together. The poem was written on one of our many visits to The Lizard Peninsula, for over thirty years a talismanic place for us, where we found renewal and good times.

Going behind the appearance of things is how Peter Redgrove described our many off-the-map jaunts to the Lizard Peninsula. For years we'd have a weekly day out over there, taking the back roads from Falmouth, swooping along by the bluebell woods of Gweek, talking about Gweek's silty river and its history. It was from here that so many economic-migrant Cornish people set sail for Australia, America and Canada, when the nineteenth century Cornish mining industry suffered a slump. Then we'd skirt Helston, that dour often rain-stricken town, before whizzing past the long reach of Culdrose Air Base and the big celestial ears of the satellite dishes at Goonhilly.

And there we almost were – approaching the pixilating lanes and roads of The Lizard Peninsula. Often we crossed the threshold into the 'Meneage', or churchland region, unable to pinpoint the exact spot or minute of entering this other world joined to the everyday world by a thin thread of serpentine weathers, a skein of blue sky.

Peter and I would often leave a rainy Falmouth and only on the approach road to the Lizard would a horizon-line of blue suddenly appear as we entered a mild and sunshiny region, though this was not an inevitable happening. I remember a February week Peter and I spent here when the fog was total; it never lifted, and in our holiday flat I listened again and again to a recording of Ted Hughes reading Four Quartets. The Lizard Lighthouse beam swung across the invisible fields and sea. The constant boom of the foghorn accompanied the voice of Hughes reading Eliot. I remember Peter and I went walking and scrambling up and down the cliff to Kynance Cove before the new path was in place, and during another stay in winter we walked at night through Lizard village and down Armada Way under a frost-enhanced star-packed sky.

When Alyson suggested a day trip to The Lizard during Storm Imogen (and what better day?) I was very much on board, but neither of us had plans to write poems about The Lizard. Our adventure was simply to be blown across Dollar Cove, to visit churches, and have lunch in a pub by a roaring fire. But I made a few notes on our Storm Imogen visit, and over the following days these became poems. I sent them to Alyson, who soon responded with her first set of poems, and another adventure had begun. We went back a month later, this time to Cury Church. Once more poems spontaneously ignited from the places and the people we met there.

More visits and more poems later, we had a book-load of them, and set about editing them during two days in the bosom of the Falmouth Hotel, to get distance from The Lizard, which we could of course see in the far distance of Falmouth Bay from the big hotel windows. A final editing session took place in London where we gained further distance.

It has been a wild and exhilarating experience. Our collaboration has been a rich, sometimes hilarious, sometimes sobering experience. Both of us have connections with the peninsula that involve personal loss and grief. The poems often surprised us; poets never achieve this by will power but through the kindly agency of The Muse (in this case The Lizard Muse) who might be obliging enough to blow some magic dust in our direction.

I'm beyond grateful to Alyson for her ideal companionship, and for enabling me to travel once again behind the appearances of things to where so many deep memories are kept safe for me. Our Lzrd poems travel behind the appearances of The Lizard, via 'the church of celtic air'.

P.S.

The Lizard: A Geographer's View

The Lizard Peninsula is a nugget of land fourteen miles beyond Falmouth, to the west of Helston in Cornwall. It is the most southerly piece of land on the UK mainland, about fourteen miles long and wide, and it tapers to a point just a mile outside the eponymous Lizard village.

Before you get there, the road will suddenly bend and swoop, buck and lean through unexpectedly deep valleys darkened with woodland on either side. When you emerge, you come into the Lizard's characteristic flat heathland.

Its flatness is not very Cornish. It is a place orphaned from its rightful geological heritage which lies to the west in Canada. Such is its particularity that, like the Fens, North Pennines, Yorkshire Dales and the Cotswolds, it is identified as a region that is distinctive in geography, geology, and climate. This extraordinary flat landscape hosts rare plants such as dwarf rush and the wild relatives of popular eatable plants such as asparagus – *Asparagus officinalis* ssp. *prostratus* – and carrots.

Parts of the Lizard are designated as a Special Area of Conservation, which recognizes the valuable habitats produced by the unique combination of complex geology and southerly location. These include its vegetated sea cliffs and Mediterranean temporary ponds. Such ponds form seasonally in the ruts of ancient trackways, but are now under threat as pathways fall into disuse.

The underlying geology and the benevolent climate support the only patch of Cornish Heath – *Erica vagans* – to be found in England. The serpentine rock, for which the Lizard is famous, was once considered to be a likely substitute for Italian marble, until its inherent brittleness was betrayed by cracked ornamental fire places. It's ideal for salt and pepper grinders, ashtrays, model lighthouses, and small clocks, all of which are produced in the village by the few craftspeople who retain the right to carve it.

Giant satellite dishes loom over Goonhilly and remind you that the Lizard has a place in the history of modern communication. This is also evident at the site of Marconi's 1901 trans-Atlantic radio broadcast from Poldhu. Among these monuments to modernity lie the evidence of prehistoric farming and human settlement stretching back as far as ten thousand years. As you tramp over the heather, the hummocks and boulders suggest field boundaries and ancient gates.

The Lizard's heathland and the wildlife it supports are protected by the National Nature Reserve, now over 2000ha (nearly 5000 acres) in size. The area under NNR designation has been growing steadily thanks to the efforts of a unique collaboration between organisations and agencies called *Linking the Lizard Countryside Partnership* (www.the-lizard.org) which includes representatives of Natural England, the National Trust, RSPB, Cornwall Wildlife Trust, the University of Exeter, and the Area of Outstanding Natural Beauty. Together, we work to protect and manage the Lizard landscape.

As you approach the most southerly point from the Lizard village, the sea opens out before you and around you, sprawling out beyond the fields, beyond the edge. The sea bed bristles with shipwrecks. Seals patrol the rocky outcrops.

Choughs – a bird believed to be extinct in the UK until ten years ago – wheel out and back above Kynance Cove. The Lizard's ancient history seems near the surface, its contemporary charms equally so. It draws me back for its beauty and wildness, its tranquility and sanctuary. When I visit the Lizard, I feel perfectly at home in its idiosyncratic landscape, whether I am running its coast path or cycling its lanes. It remains one of my favourite places in the world.

Catherine Leyshon – Associate Professor of Human Geography, University of Exeter, Penryn Campus.

Indigo Dreams Publishing Ltd
24, Forest Houses
Cookworthy Moor
Halwill
Beaworthy
Devon
EX21 5UU
www.indigodreams.co.uk